Table of Contents

Introduction

Overview of the Whole Process

1 – Find a Product to Promote

2 – Create a Product Review

3 – Upload Your Video

4 – Rank your Videos on Google and Youtube

Conclusion

Introduction

First of all, I want to congratulate you for downloading this book.

This is one of the simplest, most cut and dry book you'll ever read on the subject of making money on Amazon and Youtube as an affiliate.

What I'm gonna teach you ain't something new.

It has been working since 2007 (Youtube's starting dominant year) and it will continue to work in the next 10 years!

So if you're looking for that brand new method, then this book is not for you.

However, if you're interested in making a few extra dollars, say $500 per month while working 1 hour a day, then this book is for you.

I'm gonna teach you everything you need for you to make money.

On the next page, I'll give you a brief overview of how the whole system works.

Overview of the Whole Process

Before we officially get started with the lessons, let me give you first a brief overview of the whole process.

This is how everything will lay out and how you will make money.

Step 1 – Sign up as an affiliate and find products to promote

Get this one wrong and we're pretty much toast from the very beginning.

We need to find a product that people already want to buy!

There's an easy way to do it and I will teach it to you.

Step 2 – Create a product review

The second step is to create a compelling product review that not only is an informative review but also genuine and honest.

Step 3 – Uploading the video

This is the part where you upload your video and optimize it so it'll get as many views on youtube as possible.

Step 4 – Boost you rankings

If you want to double your chances of getting more views, then you need to apply some basic seo tactics to your video.

Just do what I'll say and you'll gett faster rankings on Google and Youtube.

Ok, let's get it on!

1 – Find a Product to Promote

Before you find a product to promote, I need you to sign up for as an amazon associate/affiliate.

It's free and it's really easy to get approved.

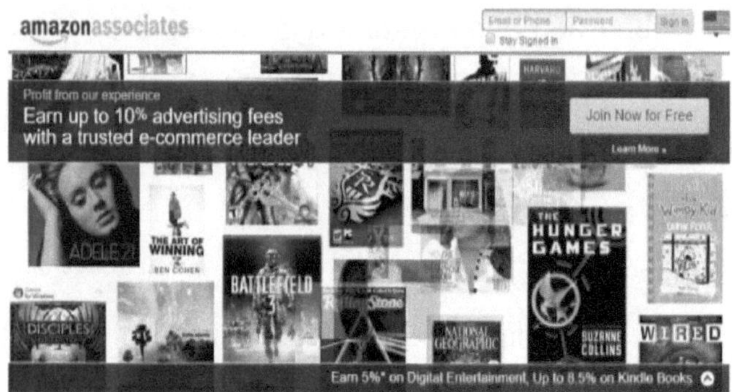

To get a product's affiliate link, you just have to do the following:

Once you application is approved, login to your Amazon associate account and click on Amazon links and banners and ***click on add product links*** now:

http://www.shoutmeloud.com/how-to-create-affiliate-link-for-amazon-product-tutorial.html

You can search for product names there and copy the amazon associate link which you will then use in your youtube video description.

If you're still quite confuse on what to do, just watch any of these videos

https://goo.gl/aOpaIz

How To Get Amazon Affiliate Links Short Codes And Long

goo.gl/wnxpYx

Or Simply type this on youtube.

Finding Products

Now it's time to find a product that we can review and promote on Youtube.

Don't make this one complicated! Cause we don't have to!

What I would do is to find a category that I'm already interested in and look at the bestsellers in that category.

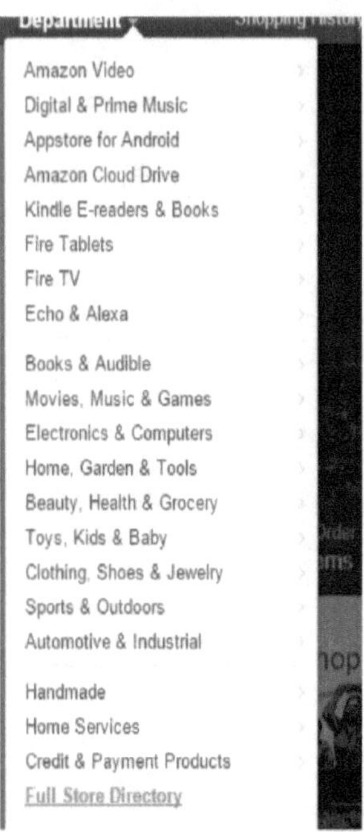

There are literally hundreds of categories on Amazon and you can choose what you want.

Once you've chosen yours, look at the top 100 and find something you are interested in.

I chose the graphics and novel category since I love reading comic books.

Here, I notice that the walking dead compendium got 3 of the top 6 spots.

This means these can be something that I can review and promote.

Also, the price is around $30 each, and if I promote all of them, that would be around $90 and it'll get me commissions of around $10.

I recommend that you promote an item that has a minimum price of $50.

Now, if you're sure that you can complement other products to promote, then you can also choose low price products.

Just make sure that it is on the best seller list and people are already buying that product.

Now, I'm sure that this product will sell if I do my product review right. But I still want to confirm it with "hard cold fact a.ka. real numbers data."

The best way to do this is to use a tool called MERCHANTWORDS.COM

This tool is $30 per month but you can easily get a 70% off monthly discount if you type "merchantwords 70% off" on Google.

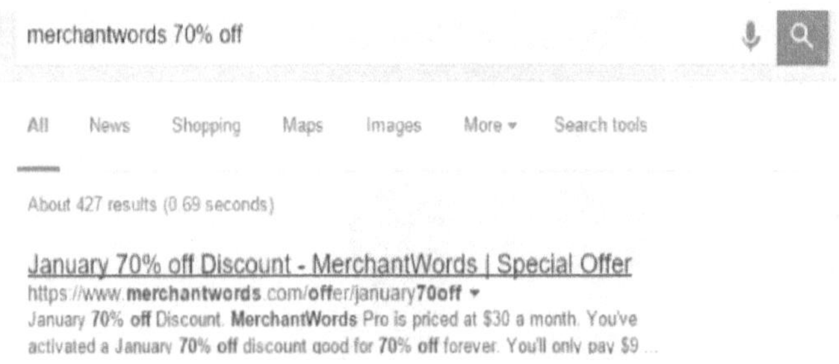

https://www.merchantwords.com/offer/january70off

This is not my link and I am not in any way affiliated with this company.

I just found this tool helpful and I use it almost every day.

What this tool does is to give you an estimate of how many people are searching for a specific keyword.

Let's say that I want to target the TWD compendium comics, I'll simple search for it on merchantwords and see if there are thousands of people searching for it.

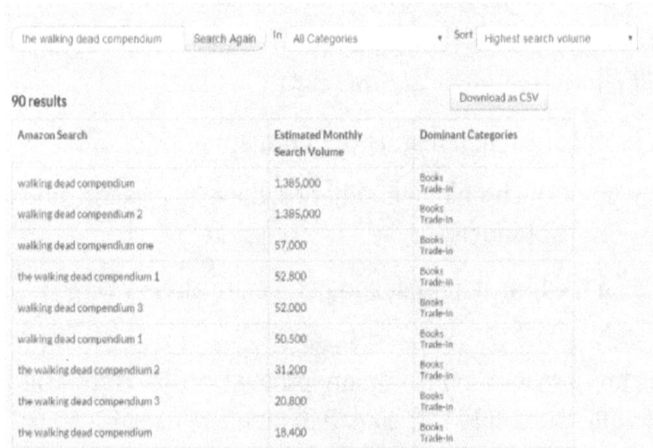

Amazon Search	Estimated Monthly Search Volume	Dominant Categories
walking dead compendium	1,385,000	Books Trade-In
walking dead compendium 2	1,385,000	Books Trade-In
walking dead compendium one	57,000	Books Trade-In
the walking dead compendium 1	52,800	Books Trade-In
walking dead compendium 3	52,000	Books Trade-In
walking dead compendium 1	50,500	Books Trade-In
the walking dead compendium 2	31,200	Books Trade-In
the walking dead compendium 3	20,800	Books Trade-In
the walking dead compendium	18,400	Books Trade-In

Woot woot!

Look at the result!

This may not be 100% accurate but just seeing the thousands of searches for this product makes me really excited.

It means there really is a market for these comics.

I can also use other searches related to the comics series and find more keyword to target for my product review.

I'll do that because I want to target as many keywords as possible.

(Why? So I will make more money , duh)

Amazon Search	Estimated Monthly Search Volume	Dominant Categories
walking dead comic	1,380,000	Books Trade-In
the walking dead comic	204,000	Books Trade-In
walking dead comics	130,500	Books Trade-In
the walking dead comics	73,600	Books Trade-In
comic books walking dead	56,500	Books Trade-In
walking dead comic 1	56,500	Books Trade-In
walking dead comic books	52,500	Books Trade-In
walking dead comic book series	49,000	
walking dead comic book 1	44,000	Books Trade-In
walking dead comic poster	43,500	Home & Kitchen Collectibles
walking dead comic book set	43,500	Books Trade-In Toys & Games
walking dead comics set	19,000	Books

Yup!

This one is a really big market I can target these keywords and use it for my video.

Once you got the product, it's time to create a product review.

2 – Create a Product Review

There is no "set in a stone" formula for creating video reviews but I have found some tactics and important things that you need to discuss in order to create a good product review.

Here are my 7 guidelines on creating a product review.

Please take note that you don't have to follow or apply all of them in just 1 video.

But the more of these you use for your video, the better your video will be.

#1 – Educate then Sell

Most people just immediately try and sell the product. They say the pros of the product and then ask them to buy it.

That's not gonna work.

There's too much competition and you need to be better than that!

The perfect solution is to educate your viewer first about the product.

Tell them the following:

What is the product name?

What does it do?

How long have you been using it?

Is it effective? Why, why not?

Have you recommend it to a friend?

#2 - Use HD if Possible

Not all of us can afford HD cameras that are hella expensive.

The best camera that you can use is the one you already have.

Use your iphone or any smartphone you have.

Most phones today have pretty good video quality as long as you find the right angle and lighting.

#3 – Say the Pros and Cons

Don't just mention the pros, that not believable. Mention some cons but obviously, don't mention some deal breakers.

Anyway, I would assume that you would only recommend something that works and is actually useful.

#4 – This is right for you if… This is not for you if…

One of the best tactics I learned from watching hundreds if not thousands of product review is that if you tell them if it's for them or not directly, they will love you and they will buy the product from your link (amazon associate url).

Have a portion of the video dedicated to telling them if the product is for them or not.

#5 – Recommend a Substitute

If the product is not a perfect fit for them then recommend a substitute product that may be a better fir for them.

By doing this, you'll get a chance to sell another product. (You'll also add your Amazon affiliate link below the video)

#6 – Tell a Story

If you have an interesting story or if you have a friend who used the product in the past. Tell them about your/your friends experience in using the product.

People want someone who they can relate to.

Don't be like a robot….

These are the pros…

These are the cons… bla bla bla

Tell them a story related to the product and they will love you!

#7 – Call to Action

Ask them to buy the product from your link!

Don't be shy in doing this. Be honest with them.

Tell them that you'll get an affiliate commission if they buy from that link.

If your review is really useful, they will use your link and they'll be happy to do it for you.

EXAMPLES:

Here are some video reviews on Youtube that you can model for your own promotion.

What is Batiste Dry Shampoo?! Report and Demonstration

https://www.youtube.com/watch?v=-_EDzRNCHq8

Dove Nourishing Oil Care Shampoo/Conditioner Review

https://www.youtube.com/watch?v=QSOXVz9up5k

DIY Teeth Whitening ♡ My Favorite!

https://www.youtube.com/watch?v=2pFAr6hgIEM

Prospector's Gold Rush Hair Pomade Review

https://www.youtube.com/watch?v=ZNHTX1qIuPs

3 – Upload Your Video

This is one of the most overlooked step of the process, especially by new affiliate marketers.

Obviously, I'm not gonna allow you to make the same mistakes when you're uploading your videos.

This step will help you get more views and higher youtube rankings guaranteed.

I'm not gonna teach you the technical part since it's pretty much self-explanatory but what I'm going to show you are the "little things" that you shouldn't forget when you upload your video.

Here are the guidelines or the most important parts of uploading your video.

A – Your Title

Make sure that whatever your product name is, that you put it on your video title.

So if you're targeting "Walking Dead Compendium Review"

Then use that keyword on your title.

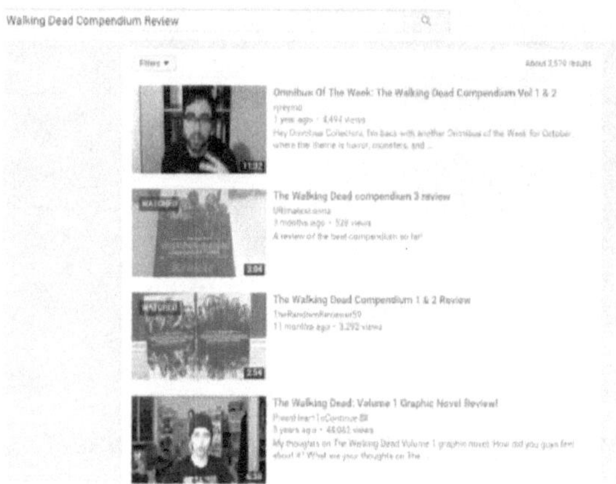

Another thing that you can do is to add words like the following:

2016 - *The Date*

Unboxing

New Review

Special Edition

Robert Kirkman – *The Creator/Author*

AMC - Tvnetwork

So instead of using *"Walking Dead Compendium Book 1 Review"* as your title, you'll use this one instead.

The Walking Dead Compendium Book 1 Review – Robert Kirkman - AMC Series 2016

By using this title, you'll get more keyword and more possible searches for your keyword.

By doing this simple trick, you'll be able to target more keywords like:

The Walking Dead Compendium

The Walking Dead - Robert Kirman

Robert Kirkman - AMC Series 2016

The Walking Dead – 2016

And many more variations that will get you more views!

So there you have it, don't forget to implement this in your own product review.

B – Your File Name

Make sure that you change the title of your file to your own video title.

Youtube will count this as "relevant content" to your main keyword (which is *the walking dead compendium review*)

C - Your Channel Name

Make sure that you pick something that is related or close to your main keyword.

Continuing our example, if you want to target that keyword, I would recommend that you use any of the following channel names.

TheWalkingDeadTV
WalkingDeadComicReviews
WalkingDeadbyRobertKirkman
WalkingAMC
TWDAMC – Comics Series Reviews

You get the point?

Use your keywords and use it often.

D - Video Tags

If you did your keyword research (remember chapter 1?), it's pretty easy to know what you'll put in this part.

Again, use your keyword and use it often.

You can also add as many tags as you want.

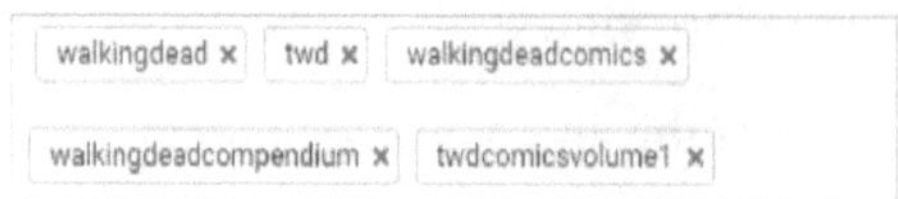

E - Description

Don't leave your description blank or with just a few sentences.

You can get more view by putting in at least 200- 300 words of content below your video.

If you can't write your own description, you can copy-paste a little bit from the Amazon listing of your product but make sure that you only copy at least half of it. The other half should be original.

And the most important rule?

Make sure that you put your affiliate link below your video!

You won't get paid if they buy it outside your amazon associate link!

NOPE:

The Walking Dead: Compendium One (Book Review) - Image Comics

ComicToyReviews

Subscribe 2,282

30,999

Add to   Share   ••• More

Uploaded on Jan 28, 2012
The Walking Dead: Compendium Volume One

Created by Robert Kirkman, this volume contains issues 1 - 48 of the comic book series.

This volume of TWD is a great addition to any collection. And for any fans wanting to try the series out, this is the book to get.

Category   Entertainment

YUP:

Published on Nov 20, 2014
How to Start Reading TWD comics Today. A beginners Guide to get started reading the Walking Dead comics and how much they cost.
Comic is sold in single issues. Six issues are put into what is called a Trade Paper Back (TPB). 2 TPBs are put into Hard Cover Books (H-
Books) and 4 HC Books are put into One Compendium which equals 48 single issues. I recommend you start out with the 2 compendiu
then move to TPB vols, 17,18,19,20,21, & 22 and pick up from the single issue #133 & #134... Then you are now caught up!!

Subscribe here for Top Quality Walking Dead Videos, new videos weekly!!

Like Make A Path Presents on facebook at
https://www.facebook.com/makeapathpre

Follow both Ronny Haze & MAPP on twitter at
https://twitter.com/RONNYHAZE

View Ronny Haze on instagram at
http://instagram.com/ronnyhaze/

Make A Path Presents YOUTUBE Link
https://www.youtube.com/user/makeapat...

Join "MAPP Steals & Deals" facebook group at
https://www.facebook.com/groups/14574...
"MAPP Steals & Deals" is a facebook group where we all post the awesome 'steals & deals' we come across either online or actu
and mortar stores! Let each other know where you see those clearance sales, bargain bins, flash sales or just some good prices for us
'entertainment merchandise' collectors! With eyes everywhere we just might never miss another sale again!

MAPP PLAYLIST

Let's Talk

F - Annotation

It is good practice to put at least one or two annotations and use it as a call to action for your viewers.

Don't spam your video with annotations, your viewers might get irritated and leave your page.

4 – Rank your Videos on Google and Youtube

Do you want to get more views?

Then you need to rank your videos on page 1 of YOUTUBE!

Here's how simple it is to do.

1. Video Distribution

Make sure that you will use your complete video url.

Go to fiverr and find someone who will do video distribution for you for 5 bucks.

Use someone with 4 or 5 stars.

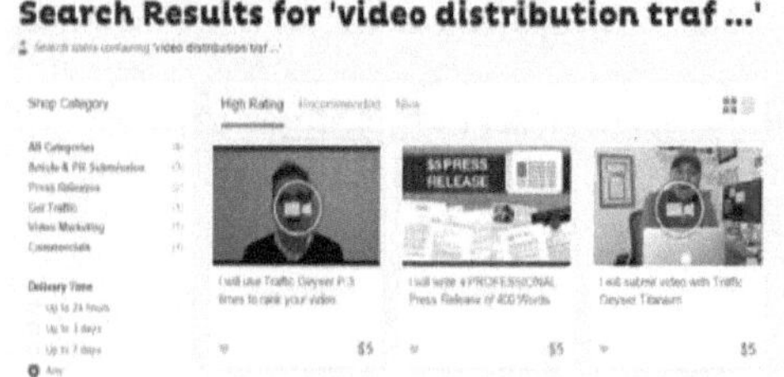

2. Send backlinks to your video

The old way is to directly send tons of spammy links to your video. This still works sometimes but Youtube is now catching up.

To counter this, we just need to send the links to a url shortener instead of sending it directly to our youtube page.

I just use https://bitly.com and put my videolink, it'll generate a new url.

You can send your backlinks in this new url.

If you want, you can tell your outsourcer to send half the backlinks on your bitly url and half on your original video url.

On fiverr, search for backlinks and find someone who can send social bookmarks or any social links to your url.

And you're done. Simply repeat the system over and over again.

Once you've done these 2 steps, you'll rank higher in Google in 2 weeks or less.

SOME ADVANCE TACTICS

USING CLICKBAIT

If you type YACHT MASTER 2 (a rolex watch) on Youtube, what video you are most likely to click?

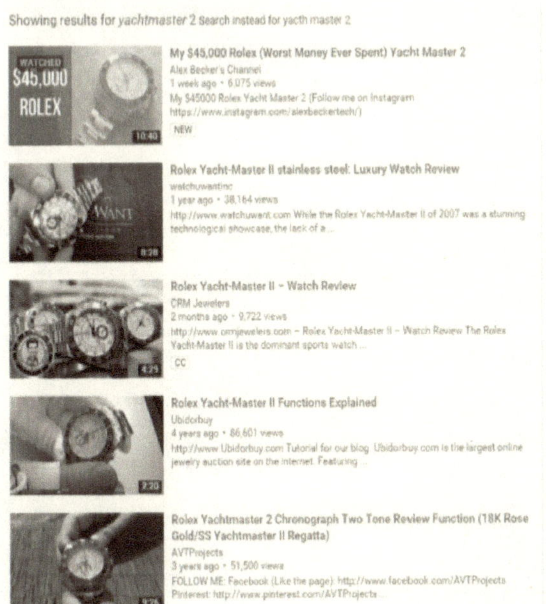

It's probably the first video from Alex Becker Channel.

Why? Is it just because it's number 1 on Youtube?

NO!

You'll click it because of the title.

That's what a CLICKBAIT is for!

So if you're selling a product on youtube, you can add some word like the following:

Product Name Review – Worst Product Ever?

Product Name Review – Better than (competing product)

Product Name Review – Worth the Price?

Product Name Review – Inside the Members Area

Use CLICKBAIT and you will dramatically increase your video views. Also, the more people watch your videos, the better your rankings will be.

Search for keywords related to your product

And then add them to your TAGS.

By doing this, you'll be able to expand your reach and get more views.

Go to https://adwords.google.com/KeywordPlanner

Then type your product name or product keyword.

You'll get hundreds of keywords related to your product.

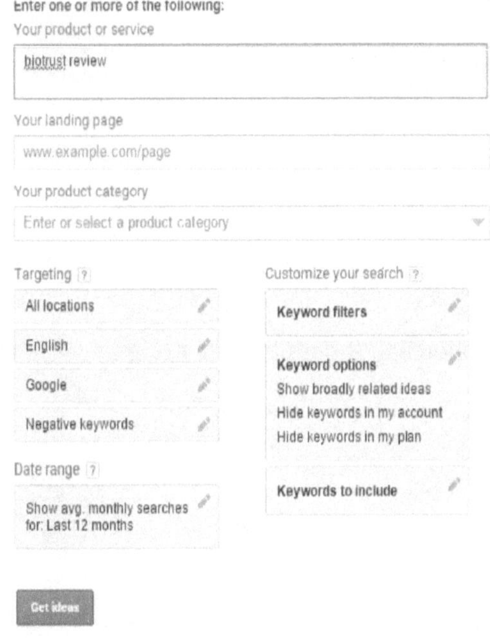

Keyword (by relevance)		Avg. monthly searches [?]	Competition [?]
biotrust		18,100	Medium
biotrust nutrition		3,600	Medium
leptiburn		6,600	Medium
biotrust reviews		2,400	Medium
pro x10		880	High
ic-5		2,400	Medium
biotrust ic-5		1,000	High
biotrust ic-5 reviews		210	Medium
ic5		1,900	Medium
biotrust leptiburn		1,600	High

Put this in your tags, product description and if possible, your title.

Conclusion

Thanks for reading this book.

I know a lot of ways to make money online but this has got to be one of the fastest and easiest ways to do it.

Now, I'm in danger of sounding like this is a get rich quick. It's not.

In order to make this work for you, you have to actually take action and do the things that I taught you to do.

You only really have two choices.

You can move on to the next "make money online" book or you can apply what you learned here, make a few mistakes and eventually make money.

I wish you'll choose the latter.

Good luck!

Norman Franklin

Fulfillment by Amazon

How to Find, Outsource, Private Label &
Sell Products on Amazon

Carl Santorini

w/ John Anderson

TOC

Introduction

Account Creation

Step 1 – Finding a Profitable Product

Step 2 – Product Research & Evaluation

Step 3 – Finding a Supplier

Step 4 – Writing a Product Listing

Step 5 – Facebook Product Advertising for Beginners

Conclusion

Copyright © 2016

All rights reserved. No part of this publication may be reproduced, distributed, or transmitted in any form or by any means, including photocopying, recording, or other electronic or mechanical methods, without the prior written permission of the publisher, except in the case of brief quotations embodied in critical reviews and certain other noncommercial uses permitted by copyright law.

Introduction

I'm going to show you a step by step plan on how you can make money by selling products on Amazon and other platforms via AMAZON PRIVATE LABELING. There's probably a million more ways to do it but I believe that if you follow the system that I will lay out to you, then you will make money.

As much as I wanted to guarantee that you will make a million dollars, I won't. Every business out there requires effort, a bit of investment and a lot of hard work to succeed. If you're in the PRIVATE LABELING business to get rich quick, then I'm sorry to tell you but this is not a get rich quick. However, if you're willing to take a few hours a day to work on your business, then you'll have a higher chance of succeeding.

Also, I wrote this book with the hope that it'll help guys like you quit their full time job. If you already quitted and you're already making an income online, well congratulations! If not, this book has the potential to help you do it.

What can you expect in this book?

Expect this book to be 90% actionable content. Most books out there about FBA are full of theories! They just want to get longer pages so they can sell their books at higher prices.

 I'll be honest with you, I have no idea if this book will be 30 pages, 60 pages or 160.

What I know is I'm going to put everything that you need to at the very least get started in this business and have a good plan of attack for your business.

I hope that I can achieve that in this book.

Who shouldn't read this book?

If you are an information collector, please, stop reading, this book is not for you. If you are afraid of taking a bit of risk and afraid of failure, stop reading also, this book is not for you.

However, if you are ready to read and implement, continue reading because this book is for you.

For you to understand the whole process much better, in the next chapter I'm going to give you a sort of 1,000ft overview of the system.

You're going to learn what to do first, second, third and on and on.

Ready? Let's do this.

Here are 3 reasons why I would rather private label a product than to buy and sell different items online.

1 – Scalable
Unlike arbitrage buying (low) and selling (high) different products – you're not at the mercy of the original product seller. What if the store run out of that product? Then you're toast!

2 – Sustainable
Since you are building a brand, you are more likely to stay in the business.

3 – Million Dollar Exits
No branding means no company sale. If you are doing arbitrage, dropshipping and other methods, it is unlikely that others will want to buy your company since they can easily find the same product you are selling. If you have a private label business, it is less about the product than it is about the brand.
In the next page, I'll show you the exact step by step blueprint to making money via selling private label items on Amazon.

Step by Step

Here is the exact blueprint that you can follow in order to make a full time income via Amazon Private Labeling.

1 – Seller Account Creation
First step is definitely the easiest; you just have to create a seller central account.

2 – Product Ideas
The 2nd step is to know what makes a great product great, so you don't have to waste a lot of time and money evaluating products. Think of this as the pre-evaluation part.

3 – Product Evaluation
The next step is to find products that will sell constantly.

4 – Product Sourcing
Step # 4 is to find suppliers for your chosen product.

5 – Product Listing Formula
Then the last step is to create product listing that will rank higher in Amazon's search engine and most especially create a product listing that will convert into sales.
So that's the whole blueprint, without further ado, let's get started!

6 – Facebook Advertising

You'll also learn some basics about Facebook Advertising.
This technique will require you to have at least $10 per day in marketing budget. It'll be worth it though, since there's a growing amount of consumers directly buying from Facebook nowadays.

Account Creation

Before you get started you have to know some basic stuff first.
Here are the things you need to start selling on Amazon.
You need to register for an account which is $40/month.
You can easily get that money back as long as you are selling a good amount
of your inventory.
Register here:
http://services.amazon.com/content/sell-on-amazon.htm

(not an affiliate link)
They will require you to provide some credit card details, personal
information and your local bank account.
If you are an international seller and if they won't allow you to use your local
bank account, you can use PAYONEER.COM and register for a free account.

Chapter 1 - Finding a Profitable Product

Before we start researching a product idea, we have to know first what in the world are we looking for. We have to know what makes a great product great.

Here are the things that I look for when I'm doing my product research.

1   - Amazon allowed category

I always check if that type of product is in the Amazon allowed category. Most e-commerce businessman starts with Amazon as their launching pad. You might as well find something that you are allowed to sell there.

2   – 4x, 5x Rule

The price of the product should be 4x or 5x the amount it cost you to manufacture (outsource) per unit.

So if a product is selling on Amazon for $30, then your cost per unit shouldn't be more than $7. There are a lot of added cost for doing business such as shipping, packaging, labeling, marketing, Amazon fees etc. All of that could possible total to an additional $13 per unit. If you sell your product for $30 less $20 for overall expenses, this allows you a profit margin of 33% or $10. Not bad.

3   – Minimum Sales Price is $10 , or $20 for those who want to make more money ☺

I usually avoid a product that sells for less than $10. It's quite hard to make a good profit for a $10 product. I would rather put the same energy, time , money and effort in finding something that will make me a bigger profit margin.

4   – Light, relatively small and easy to ship

This is true especially if you are just starting out in the business. You have no idea how much shipping would eat up your profits specifically for products that are huge and heavy. Trust me, leave those products first and start with something light and easy to ship.

However, if you insist, make sure first that the numbers makes sense. A good profit margin (NET) for me is at around 30% and above.

5   – Can be private labeled

This may vary depending on your preference. But if you truly want to build a real business with a brand name that you can be proud of. Then I would choose something that can be private labeled. Also, having a brand allows you to sell your company in the future for a 7 or 8 figure exit.

6 – Best Seller Ranking of less than 1,000 on Amazon (per category) (take note that Amazon have a lot of sub-categories) – Amazon Best Seller Ranking or BSR can be found on the product listing page.

Here's an example:

Let's say you wanted to sell a product on the bbq gloves niche.

If you type bbq gloves on Amazon's search product, you'll see the top 3 products. Open them and look at their BSR.

I would like to see the first product on the top 1-1000

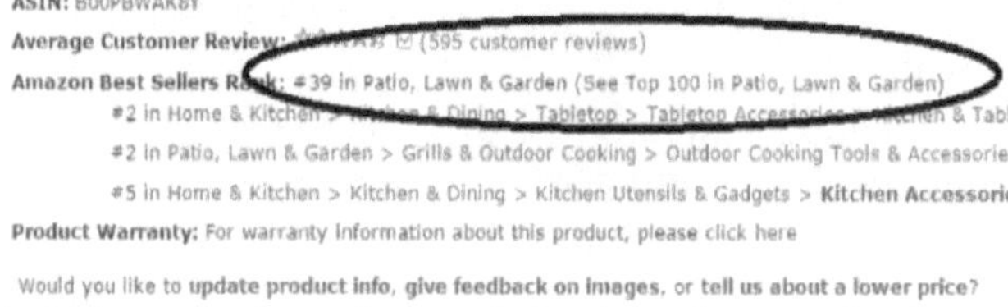

And the second product and third product on the listing to be at the top 1 – 3000

7 – It's not a "me too" product

One of the best examples I can give you is that product itself, the bbq gloves. If you look at our metrics, the bbq gloves can be a very good opportunity. But hold your horses first, this product is a "me too" product.

If you look at the search results, you'll notice that there are over 4,248 products that pretty much sell the same thing.

What's even worse is that their basically all the same product when it comes to their positioning in the market.

Look at the pictures, the way those products are sold. It's basically product after product of the same type.

Now, I'm not saying that you will not make money on this niche. If you are really good at marketing and you feel like you can outrank these products on the first page of Amazon search results, then by all means, go with these types of products. Also, if you can find a very good Unique Selling Proposition then this could be a very good opportunity for you.

Another important thing to consider is the way other e-commerce found this product. At the beginning of this book I told you about how most courses teach students to just look at the top 100 of Amazon. Well, those are your competition and most of them will be suckered into thinking that since this product is a top 100, then this must be a good product to sell. WRONG! There are already hundreds of people looking at this product; do you want to sell the same thing the other hundreds are already selling? Hmmm. Probably not.

8 – Evergreen Products

I usually avoid products that sells on a seasonal basis. I have no plan of making $10,000 on December and then $1,000 on January.

9 – Consumable*

This one is a bit optional. But it does makes sense to sell a consumable product since you'll get more repeat buyers instead of a sort of "one deal" products.

10 – I will use the product myself*

Just like #9, this one is optional. But for long term considerations, it would be nice to sell something you actually use and you really believe in. Plus it'll be much enjoyable to work.

11 – Number of reviews on Amazon for the top 3 products for the main keyword should be at the maximum of 300 for top 1 product, and 200 for the top 2 and 3 products.

If the top 3 has over 300+ reviews, I usually stay out of that market. (Especially if you are a beginner), But if you have some experience and you know you can beat them, then go on with that market.

If you are good at marketing (or if you are willing to study marketing), the number of reviews doesn't really matter that much.

The number of reviews just means that there are a lot of buyers in that market. Remember, competition is good!

12 – Merchant Words (Merchantwords.com)

I like to see my main keyword getting at least 10,000 searches on Merchantwords. It's basically a tool that gathers information from Amazon and other search engines, it's not accurate but it's close.

It's $30 per month but I'm pretty sure you can find a coupon for $9 a month. Just type "merchant words $9" on Google.

All right, I just saved you $21 per month; you might as well buy my next book about finding and negotiating with suppliers. It's not written yet, but it'll be up for sale soon for sure.

OKAY, sorry for my little advertisement there; let's just go straight to the next chapter, which is all about, organizing your product research.

13   – Is there room for improvement

If the products that are being sold kind of sucks then this could be a very good opportunity for you! You can create a better product, better market positioning and everything else.

If there is a room for improvement in that market, then that would be perfect for you.

This one takes a little bit of time and experience to understand. For now, try to understand the market wants and needs, read the reviews, most specially the negative reviews. It'll give you a lot of information about what the market wants and hates when it comes to that product.

Chapter 2 - Product Research & Evaluation

In this step, I'll teach you 3 of the best ways to find product opportunities.
Also, I'll show you how you can evaluate if a product is more likely to make
money or not.

1 - Supplier Reverse Engineering

Would you believe me if I told you that only 1 out of every 100 E-commerce
owners use this method for their research? I hope so. Do I have proof? No I
don't. But I 100% believe that to be true.

What I would do is I'll go to ALIBABA.COM, which is pretty much the
largest source of supplier's list for different products.

Then I'll go to different categories and check different products available for
manufacturing and private labeling.

CATEGORIES

Apparel, Textiles & Accessories	**Gifts & Crafts**	**Sports & Entertainment**
Auto & Transportation	Metal Crafts	Outdoor Sports
	Wood Crafts	Fitness & Body Building
Electronics	Crystal Crafts	Water Sports
	Paper Crafts	Amusement Parks
Machinery, Industrial Parts & Tools	Resin Crafts	Musical Instruments
	Plastic Crafts	Indoor Sports
Gifts, Sports & Toys	Glass Crafts	Team Sports
	Bamboo Crafts	Winter Sports
Home, Lights & Construction	Event & Party Supplies	View All Categories
Health & Beauty	Christmas Decoration Supplies	
	Painting & Calligraphy	**Toys & Hobbies**
Bags, Shoes & Accessories	Key Chains	
	Frame	Toy Vehicles & RC Toys
Electrical Equipment, Components & Telecom	Stickers	Outdoor Toys
	View All Categories	Inflatable Bouncers
Agriculture & Food		Educational Toys
		Action Figures
Packaging, Advertising & Office		Plush Toys
Metallurgy Chemicals Plastics		

I'll look at different product and just spend hours here looking for
opportunities.

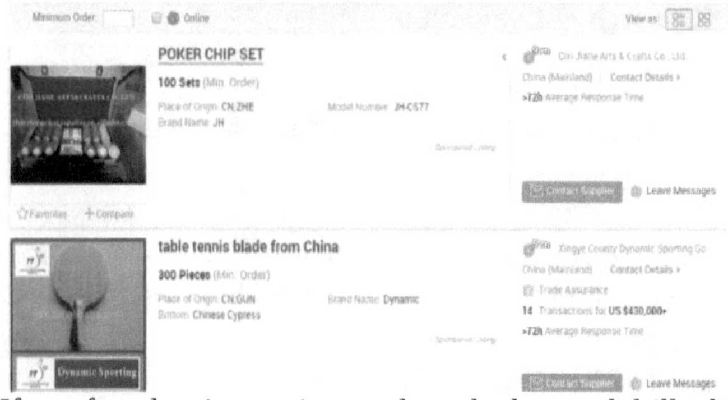

If you found an interesting product, do the usual drill which is to plug that product name in Amazon and see if it makes sense to add on our excel spreadsheet.

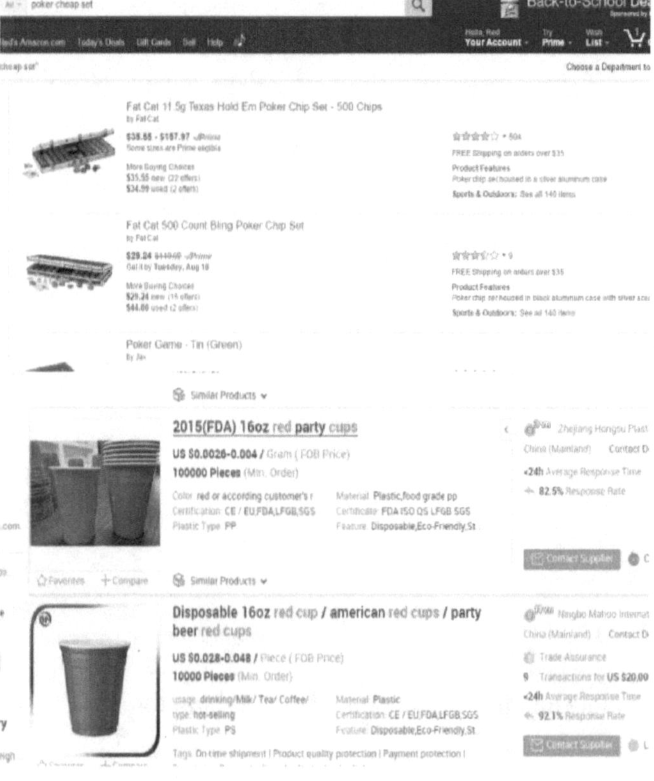

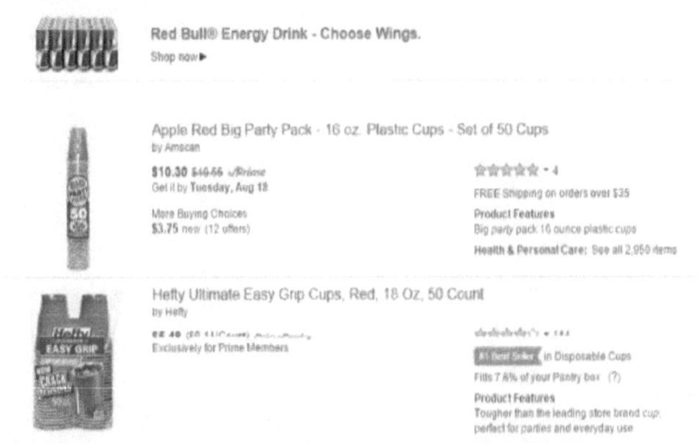

6 – Amazon Top 100

Notice how this technique is not the first tactic that I recommend? I'm glad you did. Amazon's top 100 is great but you just can't solely rely on it for research.

To find the top 100, Go to Amazon.com and click on FULL STORE DIRECTORY.

If you are a beginner, I suggest that you start with these 2 categories.
Home, Garden & Tools

Sports & Outdoors

Click on bestsellers

I would suggest that you look at the top 100 on different categories and find some products that seem to appear over and over again.

If you found that, say a water pitcher appeared twice on the top 100 best seller list, it could be a good idea to dig deep on that

Repeat the process on different categories. Don't forget to look at their BSR, reviews and other factors I told you about on last few chapters.

7 – Amazon's top 100-500

This one is a little bit tricky because Amazon doesn't really have a top 100-500 best seller list.

What you can do is to check on top 100 SUB- CATEGORIES and click on some products and check their BSR manually.

Here's an example:

In the Kitchen & Dining category, I open the Bakeware sub-category and open some product listings inside.

I click on the silicone baking cups and look at its BSR.

It's 141 in Kitchen and Dining.

If I just look at the category top 100, I never would have know that this product still have the attributes to be on my excel spreadsheet product list.

Related Searches: muddler.

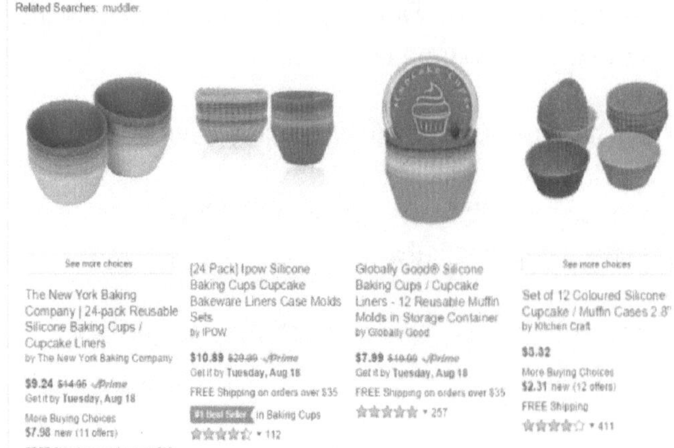

This one seem like a "me too" product (it's already saturated with the same product and same positioning for that product) but if you can create a better USP and better marketing, then this could be a great product. Don't choose this product though just because I say so. Do your own research, I gave you everything you need to find a great product, use them.

For a second thought, I think this product sucks (importing wise), especially for beginners.

Remember, use the checklist I gave you when you're choosing a product to add in your list.

Evaluating your top 30

Once you have your top 30 list, it's time to evaluate and make it as small a list as possible.

I will make the evaluation process really easy for you.

You just have to answer the questions related to our preferences and you'll be on your way to choosing a profitable product.

The evaluation process will be broken down into 2 parts.

First evaluation and final evaluation.

For your first evaluation, you just have to answer YES and NO to the following questions.

1 – Does it have private label potential? (Answer should be YES)

2 – Can it be sold for at least $10? (Answer should be YES)

3 – Will it be expensive to ship? (Answer should be NO)

4 – Is it durable and not prone to breakage? (Answer should be YES)

5 – Is it in the Amazon allowed category? (Answer should be YES)

6 – Is there any potential to sell related items in that niche? (Answer should be YES)

7 – Is the sales price x4 or x5 your Cost of goods sold?? (refer to the 4x,5x rule) (Answer should be YES)

8 – Is the BSR for the top 1 product on the top 1 – 2,000 for that category. (Answer should be YES)

If the product miss one or two at max, then throw it away. Well don't throw it away, you might still use it in the future.

Once you got the answer for these questions and you have evaluated your product, you'll probably come up with a list of less than 10 or maybe even less than 5 if you really did the grunt work on the product research part. In fact, you probably don't even have to do this final evaluation if you already have a top 3.

Now, this is where the magic happens. This is where the rubber meets the road, where the pedal hits the metal, where Ronda Rousey knocks out Floyd Mayweather Jr. cold.

It's time to know the sales potential for all of these products.

Determine first the top 5 keywords use by your competition, What are the possible keywords that they are using so that customers in Amazon will see their product listing.

If it is a product about making pop molded ice cream, then the answers would be…

Pop molds
Ice cream molds
Pop mold silicone
Pop maker
Popsicle maker
Now, how can you come up with these keywords?
Well, you can use tools like keyword Google planner and merchant words.
Here are things to consider when you're trying to evaluate your top 3
products.

- Your 5 keywords should get at least 30,000 – 50,000 in total searches on Merchant words
- There's a variety of price points
- High BSR – 1-1000
- Reviews are quite low for top 2-5 products (means there is room for improvements)
- No more than 2 products with 300 plus review (again, this depends if you know marketing)
- Consistent average review for most listings – also means there are improvements that you can make for that product – that's a good opportunity)
- I will also look at "Google Trends" to see if this product/market is on the rise or if it is a bit outdated already.

Study your niche and the overall feel of your market. Then follow the guidelines I gave you above.
Once you got your top 3, it's on to the next step.

Chapter 3 – Finding a Supplier

Most people get stuck on this part, don't be most people! Understand that once you complete this part, then you are way ahead of the pack.
Here are 4 of the best ways to find suppliers. I recommend that you start with the first technique, then if you still can't find your preferred supplier, you can then try the other methods.

This is probably the most important chapter in this book. Why? because this is the part where most people give up! A lot of newbies have a hard time finding products that they can sell for a profit. I must admit, the beginnings will always be the hardest because you still have to get a feel of your market. But once you're *"battle tested"* and more experienced, you'll find this step much easier.

I'm going to teach you six ways to find products. These are the same methods that I use every day in finding great products. You don't have to do all of them at once (that would be crazy), you just have to pick one and focus on that for a few days or weeks till you find a good product that you want to target.

The product that you will choose will always depend on how much you want to earn. If you want to earn $10 sale then obviously, you can't choose a product priced at less than $30. I found that net profits (profit after advertisements, shipping, other fees etc) are usually at 30%-50% of the total sales revenue. Don't be afraid to start small though.

Method # 0 - The non-obvious - obvious method , also, a note on Private Labels and how to find them.

You will hate me for even including this in the book, but it has to be mention.

The first method is by doing a google search, I know... duhhh..
But I see a lot of newbies don't do this. I have no freakin idea why.

What you can do is to think of a product that you want to sell, say green juice powder. You simple type on Google " Green Juice Powder Manufacturer".

Another awesome search would be… "Green Juice Powder Suppliers" and my favorite… "Green Juice Powder *PRIVATE LABELS*"

The next thing that you should do is to compile a list of manufacturers and then email or call them. Not all will have what you need, or maybe the price is not right, whatever. Just continue to talk to manufacturers to also get a bit of experience on negotiating with suppliers.

On Private Labels...

Private labels are basically unbranded finished formula or product which you can brand as your own. You just have to choose the formulas and put your own brand and VOILA, you now have your own branded product.

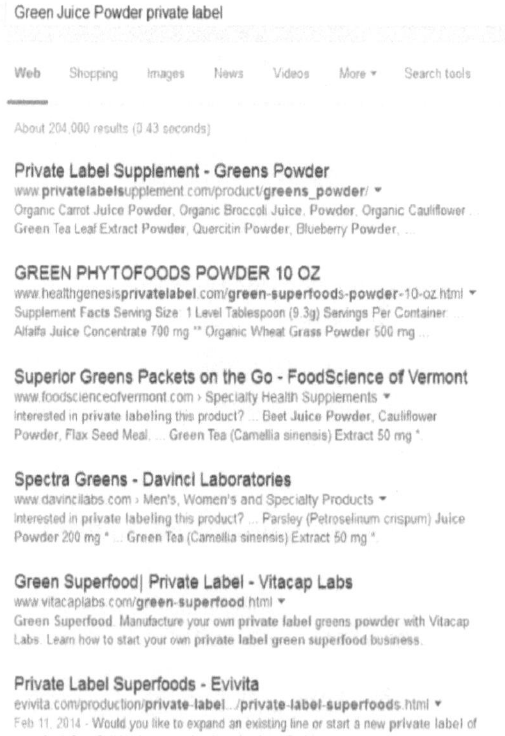

How To Find Private Labels/How to find products and suppliers

Method # 1 - Alibaba

http://www.alibaba.com/private-label-manufacturers.html

Alibaba is one of the most common ways to get Private Label Products.

The process is basically the same with WWB. You find a supplier, a product and contact them.

Beware though, some suppliers really sucks...sorry, there's just no word to describe their products and services,,.. it sucks. I'm not saying that you couldn't find a decent supplier on Alibaba, but I tend to find quality suppliers on WWB more often.

Here are some guideline to follow for you to find great suppliers in Alibaba.

Response Rate

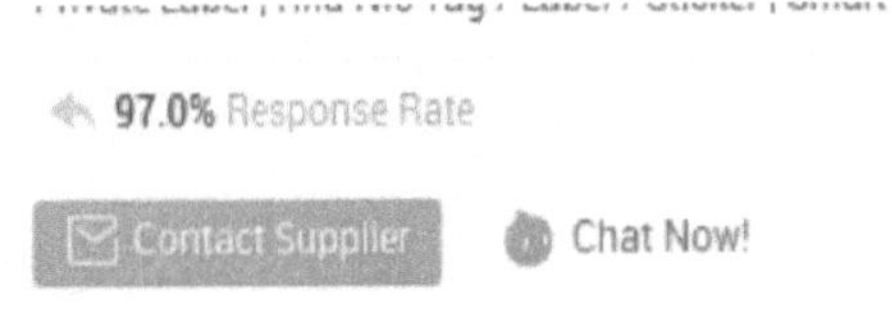

Higher response rate means they actually care about their customers.

Gold Supplier Badge

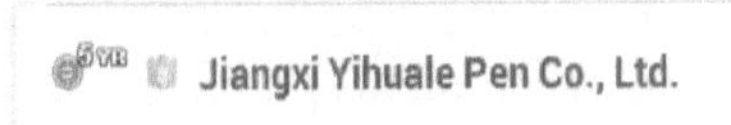

Some companies who have longer gold badge tends to provide better products and better deals.

On Time Shipment

Jiangxi Yihuale Pen Co., Ltd.

You always want suppliers who ship their products on time.

If you really wanted to private label your products, I recommend that you spend a few hours talking to as many private label companies as possible. You never know when you gonna find the best deal.

Having a Private label product gives you an identity, a brand that you can market and build, which sells you more products in the long run. It does have a higher cost compared to just re-selling products first. If you're just getting started and have no cash. I suggest that you start with the 4th or 5th method that I will teach you.

So how do you know if a supplier is a WINNER or a LOSER?

They must be in this list

http://www.npainfo.org/NPA/EducationandCertification/GMPCertification/G]hkey=a08e5382-f52b-41a7-98a9-ee40aa93aba2

http://info.nsf.org/Certified/GMP/Listings.asp

It's a list by NPA where they certify the best of the best and those who follow their regulations.

Look for feedback

You can also try to search for people who have tried their products. maybe you have an old friend who runs his own private label business. Catch up with him and ask for their opinion. Also, you can attend marketing events by people like you who wants to sells on Amazon or are already selling on Amazon. Also, a google search for that company will go a long way.

Warning: Never, ever order a full batch of products (usually $5,000 - $20,000) unless you have already tested the market.

Re-selling

Alibaba can also be used for reselling products.

For alibaba, what I usually do is just go through different categories and find different products.

I decided to go for baby products

Now, on Amazon I found a product that is selling quite well.

This one sells for $44.99, What you can do is find similar products on Alibaba. Again, it doesn't have to be exactly the same, but it has to be good quality product. The rationale behind it is that if people are buying that kind of product on Amazon, then you can probably sell the same "type" of product as well.

Look at what I found,

This one sells for $2-$5 per piece when you order them.

You can probably sell it for $20 a piece.

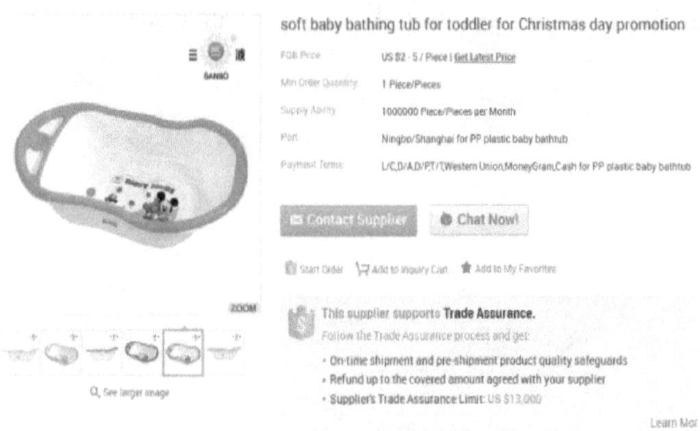

Just rinse and repeat the process. Not all products will be gold, you just have to keep digging and maybe you'll find one that will make you the most profit.

Method # 2 - Ebay

One of the best ways to profit in Amazon is to find undervalued products on Ebay. Some people might think that Ebay is dying, Ha! they are wrong, there's still a lot of people making money on Ebay. It might not be as profitable as before, but it's still a money maker for smart marketers.

What you can do is rebrand a product by taking better pictures on different angles and having better packages.

Also, don't be afraid to sort of change the strategy by buying on Amazon and selling on ebay instead. If you found an opportunity to profit, go on and take advantage of this. Some products are much cheaper in Amazon compared to Ebay and vice versa.

How to find awesome products on Ebay

Once you chose your plan of attack (chapter 2), go to ebay and find products that are similar to your chosen market.
Let's say I decided to go target "women's accessories" on the top 2,000.

I found this one on ebay selling for $9.60 per piece.

What I'll do next is find similar products on Amazon that sells for a higher price.

Please note that it doesn't really have to be the same product. It just have to be a bit similar. If that product is selling on Ebay, then it must be selling also on Amazon.

The 4th item below seems similar to the one on Ebay but not really the same. It's selling for $15, we can make a good $3 profit per item. Not a lot but if you can sell just a piece a day, that's an extra $90 a month. It can add up pretty fast especially if you're selling a bunch of items in that niche.

Now, we are not sure if that item is going to make sales because it's not really a best seller, but still, I hope that you get the gist of the ebay method.

Here's another example, but instead we're going to sell on Ebay.

search term : remote control helicopter

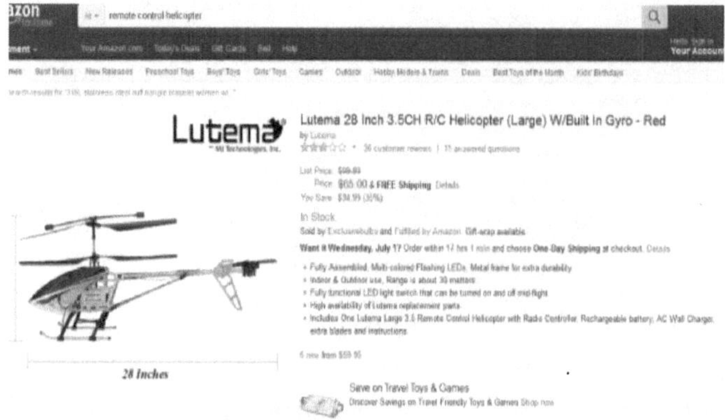

It sells for $65 on Amazon

And on Ebay… $80 per item.

Do you think you could make a profit by doing this alone? Of course.

Method # 3 - Walmart
http://www.walmart.com (go to the website and look for discounts)

Another awesome source of products is walmart. It's cheap and they give free shipping. What I do is find sales and discounts and then make sure that there is a market for it on Amazon.

Ex.

I found this on a discount on Walmart

When I searched for charcoal grills on Amazon, I found the one below.

This one is almost the same product (in fact, the one from walmart is much bigger and cheaper)

This sells for $32, I would like to think that I can make a profit by buying the $22 product on Walmart (w/ free shipping) and then sell it on Amazon for $32 or more.

Here's another example.

I found this one on the VALUE OF THE DAY tab.

$12⁹⁹

List price $30.99 You save $18.00

Coleman Sevylor Specialists - Two-Person
Inflatable Boat

★ ★ ★ ★ ★ (0)

Quick Look

it sells for $12.99

And if you search on Amazon

"coleman inflatable boats"

you'll see that it sells for $46.71

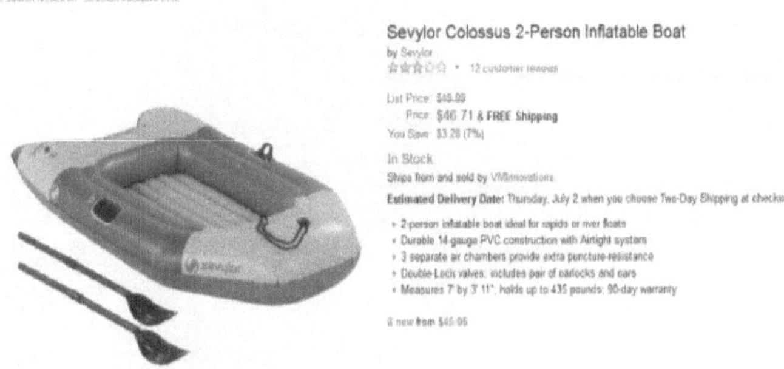

If find something similar to that and sell it for $30, you would still be able to make a good $10-$15 profit.

I hope that I have expanded your imagination when it comes to finding products. It is probably the most important skills to master if you want to succeed in this business.

4 - TTNET

I love this resource. They can give you a lot of different products to choose from and different choices of the product's origin country.
Simply search for your product and you'll find a lot of suppliers ready to talk to you via email/chat/phone.

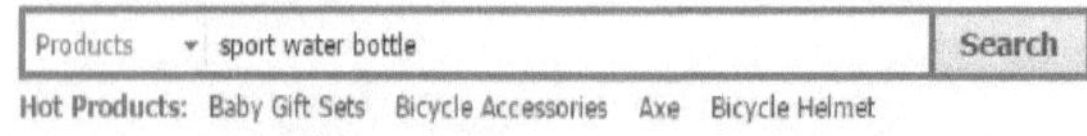

If you want to search by country or categories, you can simply choose one and go on with your research.

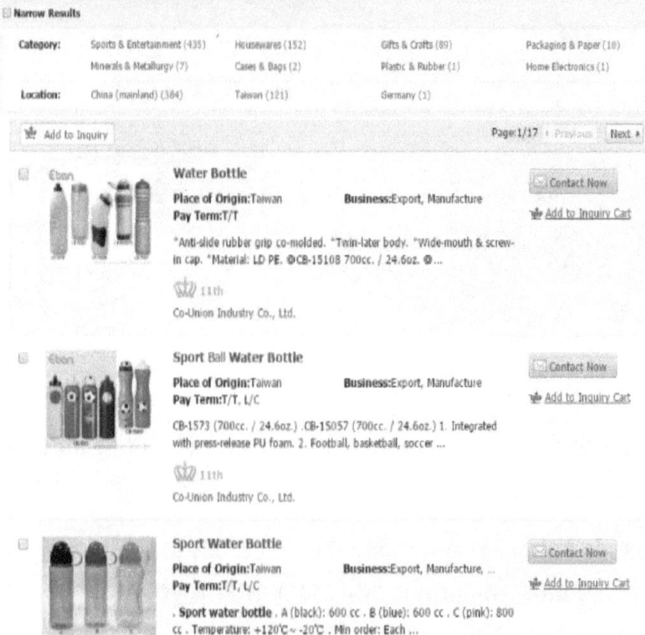

When you are looking for a supplier, make sure that you only deal with the MANUFACTURER and not a trading company.
Like this one (I can't confirm it but this one is not a direct manufacturer, they're just wholesalers)

Sports Water Bottle

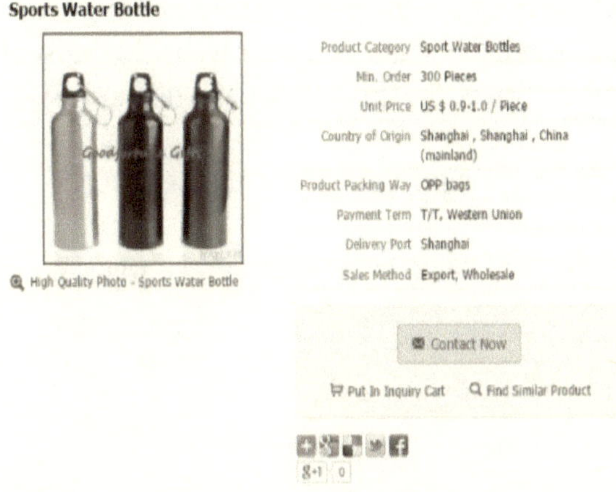

Product Category	Sport Water Bottles
Min. Order	300 Pieces
Unit Price	US $ 0.9-1.0 / Piece
Country of Origin	Shanghai , Shanghai , China (mainland)
Product Packing Way	OPP bags
Payment Term	T/T, Western Union
Delivery Port	Shanghai
Sales Method	Export, Wholesale

✉ Contact Now

🛒 Put In Inquiry Cart   🔍 Find Similar Product

High Quality Photo - Sports Water Bottle

AGAIN, ONLY DEAL WITH THE MANUFACTURER.

Wholesalers & Trading companies will add 15-20% to your total Cost of goods sold. Not cool.

In the product listing, you will see their company name.

Always open this before contacting them.

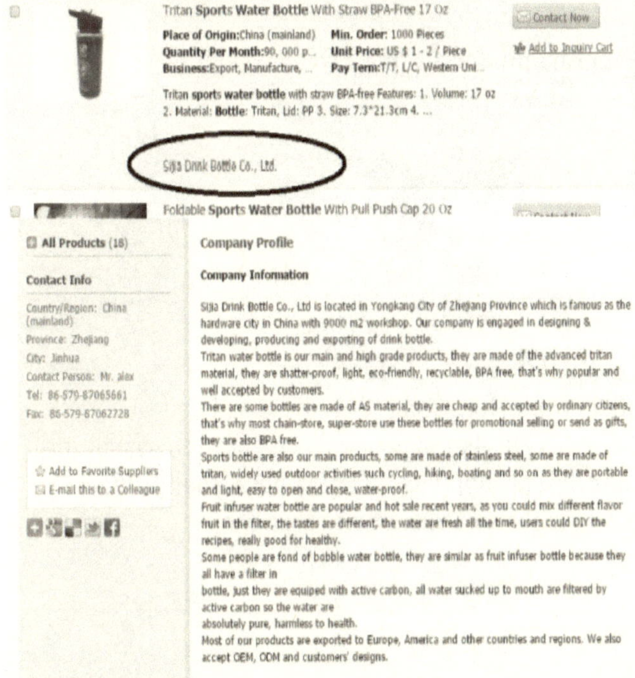

Tritan **Sports Water Bottle** With Straw BPA-Free 17 Oz

Contact Now

Place of Origin: China (mainland)   **Min. Order:** 1000 Pieces
Quantity Per Month: 90, 000 p...   **Unit Price:** US $ 1 - 2 / Piece
Business: Export, Manufacture, ...   **Pay Term:** T/T, L/C, Western Uni...

Add to Inquiry Cart

Tritan **sports water bottle** with straw BPA-free Features: 1. Volume: 17 oz
2. Material: **Bottle:** Tritan, Lid: PP 3. Size: 7.3*21.3cm 4. ...

Sija Drink Bottle Co., Ltd.

Foldable **Sports Water Bottle** With Pull Push Cap 20 Oz

All Products (18)

Contact Info

Country/Region: China (mainland)
Province: Zhejiang
City: Jinhua
Contact Person: Mr. alex
Tel: 86-579-87065661
Fax: 86-579-87062728

☆ Add to Favorite Suppliers
✉ E-mail this to a Colleague

Company Profile

Company Information

Sija Drink Bottle Co., Ltd is located in Yongkang City of Zhejiang Province which is famous as the hardware city in China with 9000 m2 workshop. Our company is engaged in designing & developing, producing and exporting of drink bottle.

Tritan water bottle is our main and high grade products, they are made of the advanced tritan material, they are shatter-proof, light, eco-friendly, recyclable, BPA free, that's why popular and well accepted by customers.

There are some bottles are made of AS material, they are cheap and accepted by ordinary citizens, that's why most chain-store, super-store use these bottles for promotional selling or send as gifts, they are also BPA free.

Sports bottle are also our main products, some are made of stainless steel, some are made of tritan, widely used outdoor activities such cycling, hiking, boating and so on as they are portable and light, easy to open and close, water-proof.

Fruit infuser water bottle are popular and hot sale recent years, as you could mix different flavor fruit in the filter, the tastes are different, the water are fresh all the time, users could DIY the recipes, really good for healthy.

Some people are fond of bobble water bottle, they are similar as fruit infuser bottle because they all have a filter in
bottle, just they are equiped with active carbon, all water sucked up to mouth are filtered by active carbon so the water are
absolutely pure, harmless to health.

Most of our products are exported to Europe, America and other countries and regions. We also accept OEM, ODM and customers' designs.

Read everything that you can about this company, especially if you plan to do a lot of business with them.

It would also be smart to Google search them and find their websites. Most of these guys in TTNET don't show their website. So you have to do more research.

Also, it would be nice to know their specialty. You only want the best and your customers deserve only the best.

If you don't have a product idea yet, you can reverse engineer the website and look for different items.

You can also email support and ask for their best categories or the categories with the most suppliers. More products in a certain category just mean more people are looking for it.

6 – HKTDC

Another awesome place to find products is HKTDC.

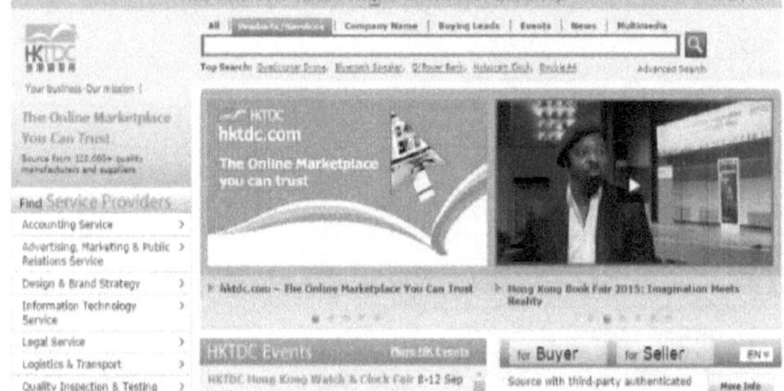

They have a lot of suppliers from Hongkong, China and Taiwan.

It's pretty much the same as TTNE, but bigger, you just have to search for your product and look at different suppliers that may have your product.

When you do your research, make sure that you tick on the MANUFACTURER only.

You may also want to consider the "credentials" bar and check out their certificates and verifications. It's really hard to explain all of it in details but I suggest that you ask customer support to explain this to you. I swear, it's worth asking and taking 15 minutes of your time to read all of those details.

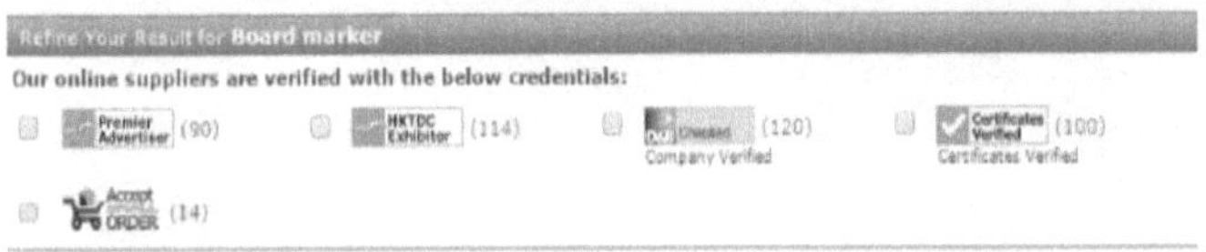

You can also click on those certifications to know what it means.

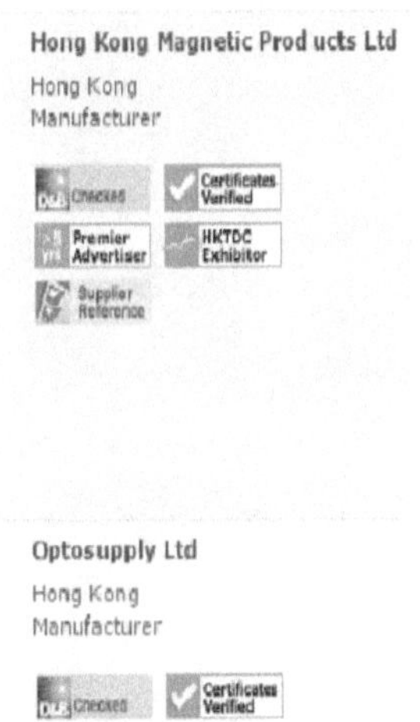

The more certifications they have,, the more likely they are to be a legit company.

Don't tick the ACCEPT SMALL ORDER button even if you're only planning to order a small amount of quantity. They will charge you more per item if you chose those suppliers. I will teach you how to negotiate MOQ later. If they really won't accept a lower Minimum order quantity (MOQ), then that's where you consider those who accept small order quantities.

 (12)

Don't forget to check more details about the company.

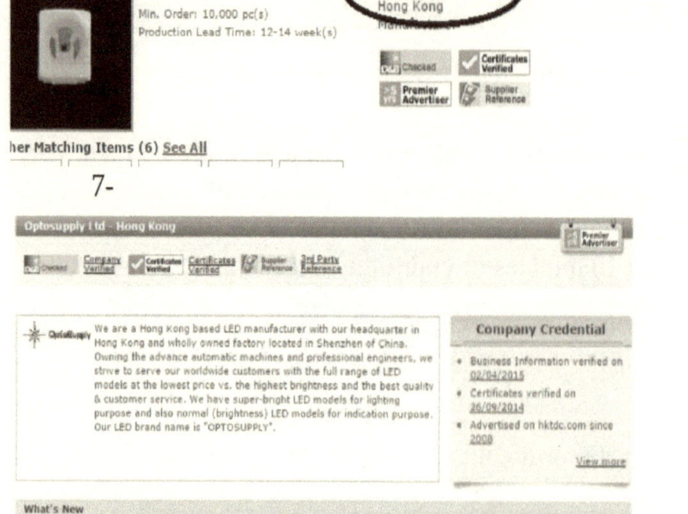

SMD LED Light

Min. Order: 10,000 pc(s)
Production Lead Time: 12-14 week(s)

Optosupply Ltd
Hong Kong

her Matching Items (6) See All

7-   >

Optosupply Ltd - Hong Kong

We are a Hong Kong based LED manufacturer with our headquarter in Hong Kong and wholly owned factory located in Shenzhen of China. Owning the advance automatic machines and professional engineers, we strive to serve our worldwide customers with the full range of LED models at the lowest price vs. the highest brightness and the best quality & customer service. We have super-bright LED models for lighting purpose and also normal (brightness) LED models for indication purpose. Our LED brand name is "OPTOSUPPLY".

Company Credential

* Business Information verified on 02/04/2015
* Certificates verified on 26/09/2014
* Advertised on hktdc.com since 2008

View more

What's New

December 24, 2011   phosphor mixer and high power led bin sorter

Chapter 4 – Writing a Product Listing

So you found a product, ordered and received it. It's now time to sell it. For you to make a lot of profits, you have to create a product listing that really highlights the best features and benefits of your product. Also, it must be AMAZON optimized so it'll appear much higher on amazon search engine.

Follow these simple guidelines to make your product listing ready for action.

Photos

Always use high quality photos. A bad photo will make your product appear unprofessional. Also, always look white background.

In addition, when uploading your pictures, change their file names into your keywords.

Titles

Write detailed product title. It helps in Amazon optimization and it makes your product stand out.

Instead of saying…

bad - Helicopter Remote Control (Red)
good - UDI U818A 2.4GHz 4 CH 6 Axis Gyro RC Quadcopter with Camera RTF Mode 2 (red) - Easy to use and control - even for kids and beginners

Make it detailed and also add some benefits.

Benefits are - *Easy to use and control - even for kids and beginners*

Features are - *Axis Gyro RC Quadcopter with Camera RTF Mode 2* (red) -

the physical attributes of the product

Description

Never rush on the creation of your description. By writing a thorough description, you'll be able to explain your product features and benefits much better. Also, it can help you rank in more keywords not included in your title.

In addition, take full advantage of the HTML amazon description feature. It helps it making your description look better and change font size, bold, etc.

Here are some basics that you can use.

B - BOLDS a phrase, used to define some words.
P - Defines a paragraph
BR - Adds line break

Here's an example on how to use this on a listing.

<p><b> Why Choose This Product</b></p>

<p> - Discraft 175 gram Ultra Star Sport Disc</br>
-The world standard for the sport of Ultimate</br>
-Official and exclusive disc of the USA Ultimate Championship Series since 1991.</br>
-Listed among the 31 things all men should own by Esquire magazine</br>
-175 grams</br>
-Foil color on the disc will vary</p>

UPC Code

Amazon requires sellers to provide a 12 digit Universal Product Code assigned for every product. This was a huge problem in the past since not every supplier provide UPC.

To get the barcode as fast and as cheap as possible, go to

http://speedybarcodes.com

You can get a barcode for $1 a piece

Home Buy Now ▾ Barcode Knowledge ▾ Barcode Questions Testimonials About Us Blog Contact Us

SPEEDY™ BARCODES

BARCODE QUESTIONS? CALL THE EXPERT
888-511-0266   307-200-480

FOR BARCODE LABEL PRICES   CLICK HERE

BIG BLOW-OUT SALE

FOR THE LOWEST BARCODE NUMBER PRICES ANYWHERE
SEE BELOW!

ALL BARCODES WERE ORIGINALLY ISSU
BY THE UCC, NOW KNOWN AS GS1-US

Chapter 5 - Shipping via FBA step by step

This chapter will be short and sweet :)

So you got your product, you've created your product listing draft. It's time to make your product available for sale via FBA.

Step 1 - Send Your Product To An Amazon Fulfillment Center

- Go to your Amazon Seller Central and create your official product listing.
- Print the labels provided by Amazon or use FBA's Label Service.
- Use Amazon's shipping to get discount or chose your own carrier if you want

Step 2 - Amazon stores your products, now ready for shipping

- Amazon receives your product. They scan and measure your product.
- Using Amazon's integrated tracking system, you monitor your product inventory.

Step 3 - Amazon does everything else for you. The shipping, the customer service etc. Just make sure that you are enrolled on FBA program.

FBA Quick Start

You can add Fulfillment by Amazon to your Selling on Amazon account quickly and easily following these simple steps:

1. Go to **Inventory** > **Manage Inventory**
2. Select a product you would like to include as an FBA listing by checking the box next to it in the far left column.
3. From the **Actions** pull-down menu, select "Change to Fulfilled by Amazon"
4. On the next page, click the **Convert** button.
5. Follow the directions for creating your first shipment.

Illustration:

source:www.amvsmlm.com

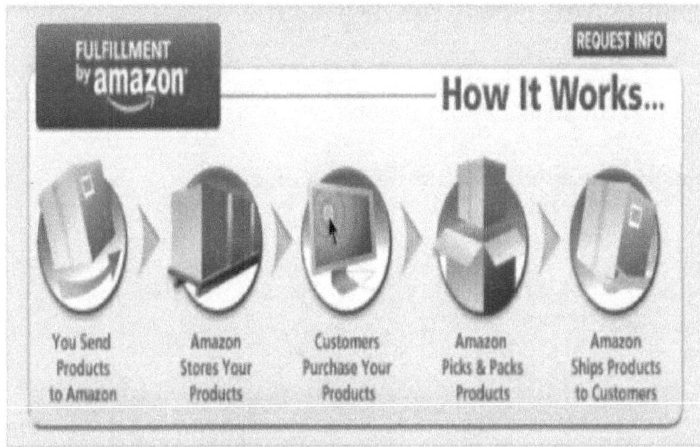

Frequently Asked Questions

If you can write a FAQ for your product, do it! The more questions you have, the better.

SEARCH TERMS

Put the top 5 main keywords that you are targeting.

Step 5 – Facebook Product Advertising for Beginners

What I'll teach you in this chapter are just the basics but it'll still be useful to you especially if you're just an absolute beginner.

You have to create a facebook page first and then create an ad.

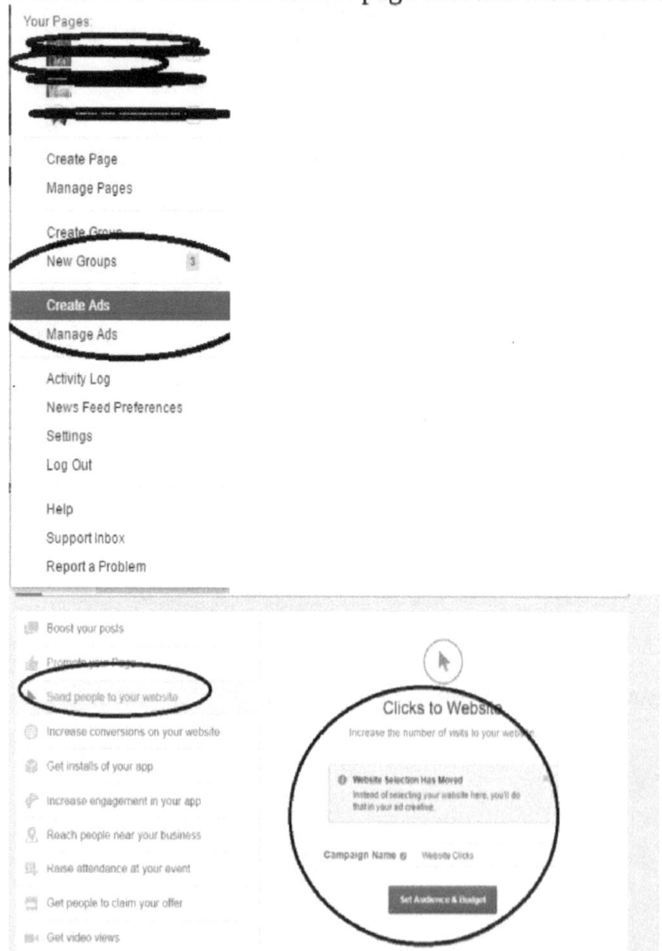

Then define your audience.

Really ask yourself, who will be buying my products?

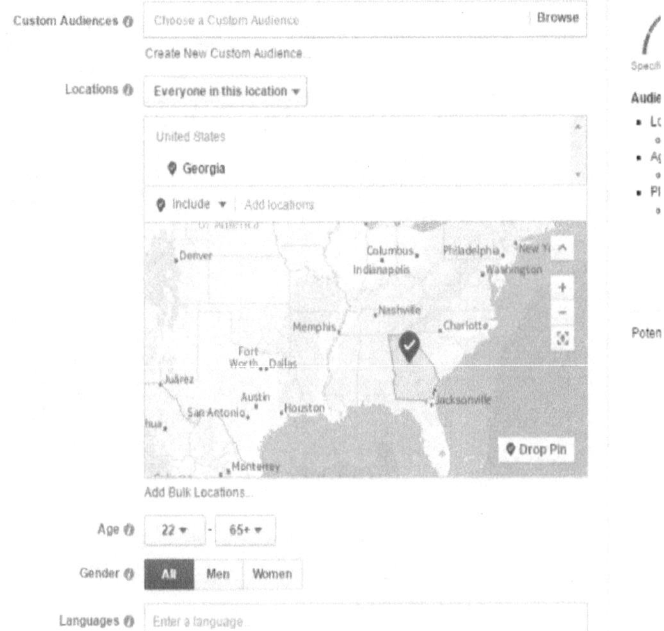

Then put some related interest.
If you're selling some Star Wars related item. Then put star wars as interest.

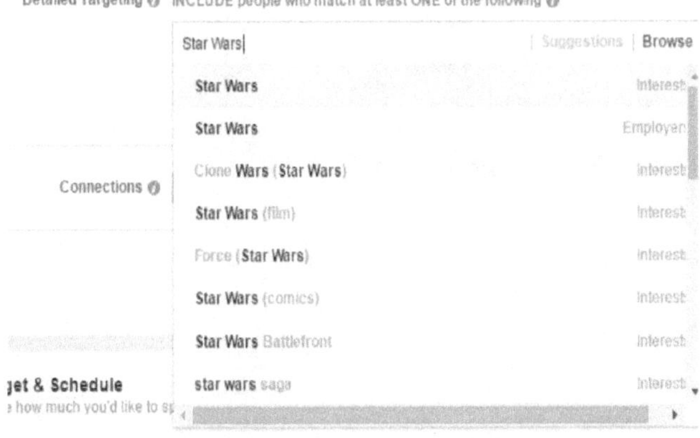

Then set your daily budget.

Leave this as is.

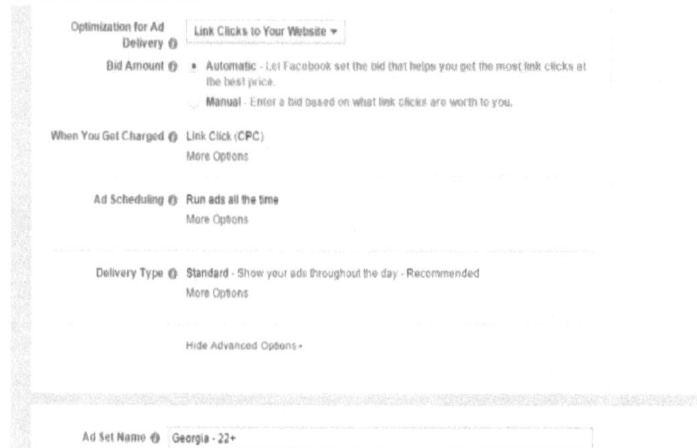

Then click
Choose ad creative

REMOVE all of these except DESKTOP.

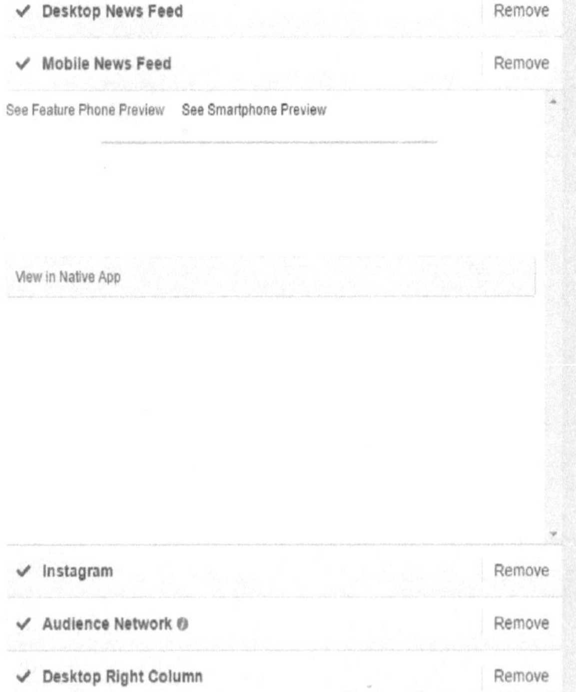

Then put your image, headline and description.

There's no magic formula for your headline and description.

Just make it as cut and dry as possible. Then put your product url.

Then place order and track your results! That's it!

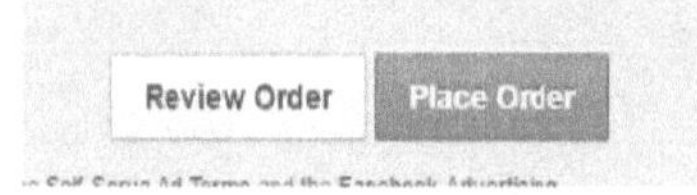

www.ingramcontent.com/pod-product-compliance
Lightning Source LLC
Chambersburg PA
CBHW031803150726
47989CB00006B/2868